Conversations with The Moon

Pablo J Castro

India | USA | UK

Conversations With The Moon © 2024
Pablo J Castro

All rights reserved.

No part of this publication may be reproduced, stored in a retrieval system, or transmitted, in any form or by any means, electronic, mechanical, photocopying, recording or otherwise, without the prior written permission of the presenters.

Pablo J Castro asserts the moral right to be identified as author of this work.

Presentation by *BookLeaf Publishing*

Web: www.bookleafpub.com

E-mail: info@bookleafpub.com

ISBN: 9789358315981

First edition 2024

Where Could She Be

I have not seen her for weeks
dreary days bring a solemn mood
the sound of the rain on the window never sounded so bad
even the willow by the river weeps for real tonight
awaiting her midnight kiss

I have not seen her for weeks
where could she be
there is no escaping this labyrinth of clouds
perhaps she does not want to be sought
and my yearning is in vain.

I have not seen her for weeks
nothing makes sense anymore
darkest nights are followed by the greyest of days
her gaze merely a memory
my heart solely an organ

Roles Reversed

I wonder if the moon came out in the day and
the sun at night
would I spend my loneliest
moments conversing with the sun
as she would be the brightest in the sky during
my darkest time
or would the moon still be there
waiting to pick up the pieces

Autumn Love

There she was
reddish brown in colour
laying atop the wet grass on a brisk November
morning
a fallen leaf yet far from broken

here I am
hanging off this seasoned branch
admiring her from above
waiting ever so patiently
to fall

Grey

I wake up every morning
In love
at peace
yet melancholy is ever so present
like the moon, deepest hue of grey: smeared in
sadness
yet effulgent and elated
In love
at peace

One Night Only

If only she would come down for one night
and dance with me
even for a moment
we could do an Argentine tango in a bar in
Buenos Aires
she would have a flower in her hair and her eyes
would be on me, only me
it would be our evening
and it would be beautiful

Summer Saturdays

No alarm
yet the birds wake me before seven
even the choir of crows sound good on a
Saturday
as I wipe the sleep from my eyes
a crisp draught creeps in through the window
left ajar in what was a sultry night

I can hear the faint sound of light traffic in the
distance
It's strangely calming
yet my attention is drawn to the sky
hue of blue lingers beyond a thin sheet of haze
fighting off the warming summer sun
awaiting to make an appearance
as am I

Miscarriage

Sat in a dark room with no windows
making small talk
hope on tenterhooks as we've been here before
anxiety strangling me with both hands for what
seems an eternity until
my biggest fear turned to reality

"I'm sorry, it's bad news today"

deafening silence swarmed the room
as grief instantly took up residence
her eyes the saddest I've seen
despair we had met before
If our hearts had voices you would hear them
screaming from the moon
and if I didn't have her I would be dead

Holiday Moon

A concoction of aftersun and perfume lingers as
a humid evening summons the mosquitos
onto my sun-kissed salty skin
my toes buried in the cooling sand

I sit back and watch the silhouette of fisherman
boats and yachts returning to the marina
white sangria in hand
sun dropping silently into the ocean on the
horizon
making way for the moons arrival
It is her turn to shine now
and I have the best seat in the house

Window

It's just a hole in the wall
no, it's so much more
the first point of contact when I open my eyes every morning
the first thing I walk up to
the only thing I look out of that shows me the exact same view as yesterday yet it's so very different today

there were more colours in the sky this morning
less plane trails
an orchestra of birds echoed down the street
The sun was brighter
I could feel the warm through the glass
this felt like a good day
so I closed my eyes and escaped for moment and felt peace

I stand here in the evenings too sometimes
after a bad day
and gaze out hoping for a ceiling of disco balls
the moon static yet slowly disappears out of view
when I was a child I would sit in the back seat of my parents car and stare at her on the drive

she would follow me everywhere
now we only have a few moments together
if I'm lucky
if the clouds are fair
and if they are I stand here by my window
telling her all of my secrets

London In Lockdown

It wasn't chaotic anymore
bare to her bones yet solemn
empty but accompanied by her memories and
the days in waiting
backpacks and camera phones on a brief hiatus
and no Veja trainers in sight

It was tranquil
a city sleeping
Big Ben under construction yet still chiming
as its bells echoed downriver reaching St Paul's

she was radiant
sun shined even brighter on her and when it
rained the groans from under brollies were hush
our chaotic streets of London were no more
even if it were just for a little while
and she was beautiful

Flame

as evening draws in
I am transfixed on this candle
its flame belly dancing in my living room
ever so elegantly
I find myself swaying with her
rhythmically
in silence

Earth

She's dying before our very eyes
deforestation so far gone it seems to be irreversible
greenhouse gasses up yearly
icecaps melting rapidly
ecosystems being destroyed
pandemics leaving people unemployed
mas animal extinction on the rise
fishing industry's sustainability all lies
we adore Attenborough for his wisdom but do many of us listen?
whilst our oceans hold the earths tears from all her crying
we ask ourselves what can we do to stop her from dying

Education

School teaches us about the wars
British and American
the tragedy of the Holocaust
and what wiped out all the dinosaurs

we are taught about prime ministers
the royal family and presidents
where mathematics is compulsory
yet nothing about social inequality

it just doesn't make any sense to me
what about the rest of it?

the colonies were not what they were made out
to be
that secret they buried under the carpet
slavery
they try and disguise a rotten history
oppression, torture, theft and murder a common
theme
locked away and never to be seen

see we live in a system where selective history
only paints half a picture

and if the system refuses to teach our kids the truth
It is our job to give them that lecture

Lonely Moon

Those days you find the moon interspersed ever
so faintly among the blue skies
and appreciate her at her loneliest,
the same way she was there for you
during those sleepless nights in solitude

August blues

The month is young, moon full
when she peaks in August it hits me harder than
the tides she turns all year round

here I am, vulnerable and eager to confide yet
she hides from me tonight
behind the safety blankets of her clouds
a night my burden is too heavy
even she can't bear it

The Playground

The playground sounds like a joyful place
for some it's just an awful place
a distant memory except the enemy still follows me

darkest of evenings spent in my room after
school mirrored the nightmare of the playground
you're too skinny, too weak they spieled
not knowing if I would survive the week
because I puked up everything they gave me to eat
that was scary
not as scary as going back to school the next day though

now I'm bigger and stronger and time has passed
scars remain of that awful past
but I'm okay
I'm fine
but believe you me I hate the playground

Routine

Children stand on heaps of dust
at home yet lost
fatherless, motherless, sisterless, brotherless

hearts and city shattered
eyes find tears from bottomless oceans
screams louder than air raids
cries louder than misiles landing yards away
where children used to play
heart-stricken mothers plead to the world for help
and people do listen
just not the ones that can make a real difference
so the bully boys next door continue to stamp
their feet with their polished boots
and the world can only sit and watch

there are no birds singing in the trees today
nothing but ringing ears and a grey sheet
covering the blue they long to see again
along with hope of seeing peace at home once
and for all

for they are sick and tired of bloodshed and
oppression that surviving this time around isn't
enough
a truce isn't enough
a seize-fire isn't enough
this isn't dejavú
this is routine

Drowning isn't an Option

Life is slow when you're in your twenties
slow, sweet, serendipitous
you have all the time in world
time for growth
time for laughter
time to wander
time for mistakes
feet of the breaks
time to live at a hundred miles an hour
absolutely no time to think
one blink, lo and behold you're in your thirties!

time accelerates
your mind wanders
plenty of time to think
and panic, and obsess
the stress of life strangles you
you can't breathe
over-thoughts and regrets of what you haven't
done or haven't achieved
yet the focus should be on what you can do
on what you can achieve, believe!

time is still on your side
take pride of whom you are

who you have grown to be
on where you want to take yourself
and who you want to take with you
let your stresses and worries take control but
positively
let them be the driving force and
reach those high places you've dreamt of
those places you've prayed for
let your heart take you by the scruff of the neck
and make moves towards those unreachable
places
you'll make it

love harder than ever
cry if you have to then
wipe those tears and smile wider
and with any leftover tears take them and throw
them in the ocean and ride those waves
stay afloat and
don't you dare even think about sinking
cause drowning isn't an option

Conversations with the Moon

sometimes I search for advice in the poetry I write
those vented words strangely bring me peace
and my endless fire that raged within moments ago
Is now a slow burn
so I set up camp
heart heavy and hunched in the palms of my hands
and sit here having conversations with the moon
who's present as always
earthy grey in colour
perched perfectly on a dark nightly canvas
guided by a thousand stars
showing me that she also has her imperfections
yet she accompanies me through this long cold somber evening
and together we work things out
just in time for dawn to break

Alone

I feel like a buffoon or a dwarf in a seventeenth century painting
humiliated, sad
ridiculed and alone in the middle of a room
where everybody's gaze meets mine

I want to scream but I am a mute
so I sit here silently and weep
hoping my tears will run the colours on this canvas
so I can disappear

Perspective

I hate who I am
and I don't think you'll ever hear me say that
I matter
I know deep down that
this is the extent of my happiness
and that
my negative thoughts define me
I refuse to think
there's a positive side to everything
I'm ashamed of myself
It's got to the point where I can't say that
I deserve to be here

Read again backwards

Milton Keynes UK
Ingram Content Group UK Ltd.
UKHW020810080424
440801UK00015B/780